DAYS LIKE THESE

A Gift for the Spirit

by

Tom McCoy

REVIEW COPY
Not For Resale
High Sierra Books
P.O. Box 489
Gold Beach, OR
highsierrabooks.com

High Sierra Books π Gold Beach, OR 97444

Copyright © 2004
High Sierra Books

All rights reserved, including the right to reproduce this book or any part thereof in any form.

ISBN: 0-9743573-0-8

First printing: January 2004

**High Sierra Books
P.O. Box 489
Gold Beach, OR 97444**
www.highsierrabooks.com

For my folks,

Thanks for all the unlearning I didn't have to do.

Table of Contents

Introduction ... ix

Part I: Dawn

days like these	1
the handsome bird	2
safe passage	3
shredded wheat	4
some days	5
gun control	6
homage	7
among friends	8
for carol and betty	9
waiting for moby	10
foreign lands	11
view from the cave	12
without tools	13
the journey	14
small boys	15
cleopatra's socks	16
visions of the faithful	17
evening	18
small birds	19
when I grow up	20
the zealot	21
cities of the heart	22
summerfield	23
once a man loved by sin	24
proper dog	25
the trader	26
fort bayard (for larry godfrey)	27
the mission	28
the bird feeder	29

the cost of roses	30
fields of summer	31
prince of winds	32
notes on the end of the world	35
expertise	36
covenants	37
betty	38
attrition	39
a house in town	40
soup kitchen	41
the janitor	42
thieves	43
the novice	44
walt whitman	45
taking aim	46

Part II: Noon

willows	49
january	50
wet weather	51
winter tale	52
the desert first	53
the wise	54
the record	55
o la love	56
the stone boat	57
midnight kite	58
composition 101	59
thinking of you *christmas 2001*	60
the ace of strawberries	61
doves	62
trees	63
observation at 55	64
to a son	65
late afternoon	66
kildeer	67

tigers	68
excerpts from the dogboy chronicles	69
sailors and unicorns	70
seraphim	71
conditions of longing	72
bird watching	73
love beyond star trek	74
elvis revisited	75
no elephant graveyard	76
monsoon	77
peanuts	78
possibly the last love poem	79
awaiting velocity	80
baby steps	81
homemade biscuits and blackbird dreams	82
the race	83
sailor	84
sunday drive	85
housecleaning and the part-time zealot	86
pale horses	87
cats dancing (for josh and hunter)	88
hard morning	89
rock soup	90
the daily log	91
country fair	92
the death of miss cluck	93
the christmas wreath	94
the snowman	95
new snow	96
plato's pants	97

Part III: Dusk

a summer thing	100
the winter child	101

early warning	102
forms of war	103
you said	104
where the free light falls	106
the dust suit	107
orpheus depending	108
bow hunting	109
hollywood the screenplay	110
the task	111
the saint	112
the way back	113
the nihilist retires	114
the midnight garden	115
things shining	117

Introduction

The reason Tom McCoy has not pursued publication of his poems prior to *Days Like These* is quite simple: the thought never occurred to him. For McCoy writing poetry is a right way of living, a kind of prayer or spiritual contemplation perhaps, a deeply personal act that is as private as it is profound. Poetry is a method of celebrating the possibility of being, as Rilke would have it, and an excellent mode of balancing the external with the internal. The idea of his work being read by strangers in strange lands, although not appalling to McCoy, never crossed his mind. Although he shares his poetry with friends, family, and the local community in Silver City, New Mexico, going beyond the bounds of his own environment struck McCoy as somehow unnatural.

Author John Gist (*CrowHeart, Lizard Dreaming of Birds*) met Tom McCoy while teaching at Western New Mexico University in Silver City. They became acquainted at a poetry reading for local authors. Soon they were spending weekends driving around the desert and mountains of southwestern New Mexico talking about nature, writing, metaphysics and the possibility of being. After a number of months, McCoy shared some of his poetry with Gist. And so began the process of Gist attempting to persuade McCoy to pursue publication. After four years of persuasion, McCoy finally agreed to allow High Sierra Books to publish the first volume of his poetry. We believe lovers of verse, imagery, and metaphysics are going to be very happy with McCoy's decision.

In reading his verse–the complexity of image, the simplicity of language, and the playfully-profound subject matter–one may wonder why McCoy's name is not associated with the best American poets. It is because McCoy is more than content to compose poems in the void of obscurity. A kind of modern day Emily Dickinson on the one hand, with a bit of a non-ambitious Robert Frost on the other, combined with a sprinkle of Kerouac, Ginsberg and Snyder, McCoy's poetry is fresh, timely, and unmarked by academic conservatism. It deserves a much wider audience. Young poets, especially, will be struck by McCoy's work. In it they will find that profundity often times hides in the mundane, the every day, in days like these.

It may be surprising to learn that the academy, the pillar of freethought and experimentation, in actuality is one of the most conservative of institutions. Most humanity departments around the country rail against innovation. It is a fact, just ask your local philosophy professor or English instructor about the stifling nature of the university. This leaves creative writing students, who are brought up to believe college is the place where they will finally be able to express themselves freely, a bit confused. Instead of embracing diversity, most writing workshops are fueled by a herd mentality–writing by committee–the end result being the will to mediocrity or attempting, in vain, to attach permanence to events that are as fickle as the ego itself. The *writing workshop syndrome* is usually associated with fiction. That it is alive and well in poetry workshops should not come as a huge surprise.

Tom McCoy escaped the workshop trap. Although he does belong to a group called *The Grumpy Old Men*, who meet every now and then to share poems and discuss technique and process, the group openly encourages innovation, individuality, and poetic license. In the end, the pursuit of any art is lonely. To touch the unity inherent in the universe, one must go it alone. Mystics, artists, sculptors and poets have known this for centuries. In an age of scientific materialism, it is time to celebrate unity one by one, as individuals, not as herds. *Days Like These*, for those who are not up to the rigors of practicing Zen Buddhism or joining an ashram, is a peek into the world of the sacred–illustrated through the mundane. It is a book for everybody and nobody, a look into the eternity of a moment, a celebration of life, loving, and death. It will mean different things to different people, but nobody will walk away from reading these pages unaffected.

With titles like *Elvis Revisited*, *Conditions of Longing*, *Shredded Wheat*, *Forms of War*, and *Love Beyond Star Trek,* it becomes apparent that McCoy is playful and serious at once. As mentioned earlier, the complexity and juxtaposition of images is sometimes irreverent, sometimes reverent, and at other times joyfully-wicked. Each poem presented in this book will strike each reader a little differently, but it is safe to say that all readers will experience a shiver or two, possibly goosebumps, a few laughs, and some tears by the time they finish reading *Days Like These*.

With that, enjoy. And remember to look for the eternal in the moment, the sacred in the mundane. McCoy is a master, and maybe along the way we might soak in a bit of his wisdom.

Wendy White
Editor

Part I:
Dawn

Days Like These

days like these

the dark relentless flower of night has held me too close
i am sotted with moon
and the jejune elegy of roses falling away into grandeur
i crave feral sonnets of heartless titanium
and the bold clacking teeth of the righteous

when gods flew close to the ground
we strove with them mouth on mouth like horny sailors
drank iambically to prove our vegetable wings
the ground was hulled with heroes

on days like these
i am content to pursue the politics of ease
and with sufficient air lecture recalcitrant chickens
and wonder if what i thought was patchouli
was another incense burning.

Tom McCoy

the handsome bird

that morning of beginning
a robust bird flew intricately from the city of blue beckonings
past the hillbilly sunflowers
the slow secrets of trees
the jack of leaves on fire
a handsome bird of immense joy and fragility
circling in the two-fisted air
singing hepsibahs and hooligans and dirigibles of delight
then lit like fire in the eye of the day

someday i hope to live that way

Days Like These

safe passage

the chicken is noble
because it does not want more than a chicken wants

i am not noble
i am a sad doctor moving down streets of wind
neither healing nor having

the chicken is noble
because it does not know it is god

i am god
but do not know that i am a chicken

i must leave this farming to the dead
or those with a better grasp of husbandry

i only know that i am a door
not a safe passage

shredded wheat

god stumped into the kitchen shaking off light like a wet dog
it fell in pools to the floor
he smiled and shrugged
we had shredded wheat and bananas for breakfast
he used a lot of sugar
his hair was black and shiny as a raven's butt
none of that white-haired windy-bearded shit
he wore tennis shoes and a t-shirt that said
EASY DOES IT
he stood up
-gotta go
keep up the good work kid-
he smiled like a tuna boat at sunset
and set off down the street spilling light and tipping over dogs

Days Like These

some days

i saw dylan thomas round as an apple
riding a spring chariot
writing fire in a book of clouds
the great dusky birds of morning
whispering hosannas of budded angels in his ears
a rainbow of stars across his shoulder
his dark eyes chattering psalms
as he passed to the west reciting muscular tercets of sea bells
while proclaiming his innocence in all matters concerning ecstasy
and dwindled to a small storm in the foothills
by suppertime

then we switched on the news
and the rain came down

some days are like that

gun control

that anfractuous lad
we flew with him
poor icarus took the fall
he fell to the gibbering sea
we went to the mall

daedelus roundly cursed the sun
learned what we all suspected
hate is love exhausted
and went to get his gun

Days Like These

homage

purple pears
o bridges of bright morning pears
o ransom of pears
red pears in the sunset
the flawless pears of evening
o see the sails of the sea are ripe with pears
high-heeled pears
pears your mother never made

the porch is covered in pears
their cooings and nuzzlings waffle the air
the moony man with runic eyes
is pulling pears from his numinous coat
quoting arias of neruda and the sublime dirges of atlantis
and reciting the thousand theses of solitude with odyssian mirth

"i have squandered the thirst of a lifetime
spent the bullion of the resinous soul
on the shoeless slut of perfection

pears come and go
but the mind circles forever the backwash of a dream"

among friends

having seen morning steal like a child
from the fields of night the molten melon of the sun
and the fingers of day spread like honey upon the undulant land
i choose to linger where friendship lies like magnificent unsmoked cigars
in the scintillant lagoon of the mind

Days Like These

for carol and betty

she bought new sandals for the funeral
in the spring when the sky falls
like judas on the myth of being
with the whispering in the grass
the shadow convention delegates kissing
like sailors behind the billboards
you feel somehow you have left something of great value
wandering the slow forests of night

this strange geometry of death
this tear in the deep curtain of the self
calls to mind a child lost in the high grass of spring

grandma's in the ground
the chickens are fed
the fat balloon of the sky rotates
night captures the town
and already you can't remember whether she liked lemon pie
but her smile is like a bird at the window

waiting for moby

always the feeling if i could turn around fast enough
to catch the old guy with his hands in his pants
my world would fall away like lemon pie in the rain
and i would step up to a better grade of applesauce
my name espaliered on fine restaurant placemats
girls would abuse me with their breasts under blazing willows
and cars would sigh deep in their carburetors at my touch
but he is quicker than a virus
holds me to his rule
harpoonless in this ticking place like a sailor in a sandbox
waiting for moby

Days Like These

foreign lands

i sent the heart scouting
down a high-backed holy wind
in a country of slow color
saying
-tender fox
seek the lost tides of longing
the long-legged dreams
our fathers foundered on-

to the elder east
among the sharp hiss of sun and moon
she flew
to the dark shades of west
and the vast undulant noon
north of night and east of belief
the intrepid heart shuttled like a sorcerer's prayer
down the salty winds of our ways
that gentle dove of engine soared
binding the world like incense
to her heart-heavy wings

and now
that solitary bird sings only
of the hidden lions of light
the bright apples of the mind
fathered and lost in our own foreign lands

Tom McCoy

view from the cave

the sun rises like a god out of the hill
as the spirit gathers on the fields of morning

buzzards score the hungry air
spying out the edges of life
and i realize
birds are my heroes
they can fly and shit at the same time

Days Like These

without tools

once the tools are gone
the man is gone

on a spring morning i think of lenny
the virtual optimist and the necessity of pliers

a man of decent lusts and graceful whimsy is gone
the world hiccups and breeds
the residue is bought and sold by realtors
and we learn if at all
to build castles out of wind
and fly the heart like a kite
held only in joy

the journey

on the way to my death
i met a woman
with fire in her bones
the wind in her smile
i stayed awhile

on the way to my death
i met a child
lost in a wondrous way
i wander with that child
unto this day

Days Like These

small boys

"if you're looking for sympathy
it's in the webster between shit and syphilis"

grandpa wore a hard hat
died with a whimper
in a puddle of his own juices

a big eyed child
i wondered about that
and the misery a loving heart conduces
and went outside and stoned the cat

small boys are their own excuses

cleopatra's socks

the day the waffle iron died
turtles on venus wept
chickens gnashed their tiny teeth
watermelons ached openly in fields
juke joint impresarios parceled free beer without knowing why
the man who invented electric rubberbands pledged his fortune
to swath the homeless in yogurt
fish stopped on their way home for a beer
as tigers wandered aimlessly through the streets of omaha
and tiny children gnawed the shins of airport hare krishna's
perhaps knowing best how we are joined by milkshakes
and bees' knees and cleopatra's socks

Days Like These

visions of the faithful

in this dominion of dogs
fleas rule
the sweaty folk lurch about
their bibled shouts
hard as nickels in the green air

the heart's braille engine sighs

once
under the winds of fabulous
were trees slow dancing
in their skins

in the city
things do not go well
the love tractors
fail to pull adam from his rib
the neophytes are up to their asses in creation
st. gizmo sags back mumbling crucifixes
his dick in the dirt

and i said

-oh lord
be a v-8 for me
a king kong mud bogger
of biblical intent
for thy glory . . .

but they were gone

such are the faithful tested
in parables of wonder
and thus comprehend
how in gospel throes of good red roses
trees waving make the wind

evening

ravens rowing home
black boats glistening in the soft sun

day gouged out
a hulk dangling from smoking threads

somehow
in the intricate dark
night fills up day
and i am blessed by the strong hands of night
waking like a thirsty child
to the tall glass of morning

Days Like These

small birds

panjandrums
morning's banquet
the exultations of small birds
anoint the heart
like a storm of roses
articulate a side of being
that has no hands or numbers
but owns more country
than all the princes of reason

when i grow up

in the tall house of morning
by the field of bright horses
i will live like a haiku
with the precision of infidels

Days Like These

the zealot

i am waiting
waiting for a feast of wings
hosannas on the half-shell
omar khayam
glistening in a ruby yacht

i have blisters on my waiting

a partial vacuum
in need of deep space
i want to be jumped by jesus
beat by buddha
killed by krishna
invaginated in the mother womb
stuck like road kill
to the wheels of his great heart

though i'll probably just go home
and rotate the tires on the ford
i'll be waiting
watching the furious air
for signs of imminent
and all-consuming grace

Tom McCoy

cities of the heart

she comes in a gathering of small birds
small winds in her wake
the room elbows out
windows smile and all the spoons ache
it is always thus

a handy man for my part
i am versed in her ways
apprenticed to the sensualist's art
we dine before we pray
in the cities of the heart

summerfield

i held a hummingbird in my hand
shimmering green skin
eyes of a small lady

it's so tired

is it dead

        dad?

no

its feet lie like crumpled
trout-sized wire fish hooks
in my hand

bumping off the porch screen
like a crazed june bug
the fear hurts

don't break him!

piled in the bottom of a five-gallon bucket
used up
a breath of a bird

something moved in me when i held it

it shivered once and flew
and i felt a joy so piercing
it follows me
down the days

Tom McCoy

once a man loved by sin

once a man loved by sin
carnal as a cat
prodigious in whim
i am become what i cannot fear
dancer among birds
in a shanty land
king of small beer

the sauntering selves converge at the known
an island in a stone

the dogs of lust grin and groan
o' love's a tipsy biscuit
i'm a waterloo of one
(nothing stirs the wanton pups
like the sound of gravy in motion)
ablaze on a sinking sea
the ocean's motion moves in we

adam's ache apples up
old loves lash me like a rose
what the sweating world sees
i would see
my heart pumps pure crow
pure crow

from nothing spring the seeds of light
(the dead kiss back the dew)

in this curved space
i learn by listening
and listening
learned a lovely thing

god listens as he sings

Days Like These

proper dog

i want a proper dog

in this world of drooling turd-sniffers
the dogs of noon with thieves in their throats
hold the day

i want a superconductor of dog
with the moon in his walk
that pisses pure silver
whose bite is his bark
not politician dogs
that shit one day and eat it the next
hindy licking lawyer dogs
insurance dachshunds
real estate poodles
pit bull bankers

i want a dog of the people
a morning dog with no coffee
to tell me straight out which way the heart is

the trader

lately
i have become enamored of elbows
and the vastness of sunflowers
having traveled far through clouds of fierce bedouins
with twangy nose hair
they all wanted my cigarettes and velvet paintings of elvis
their eyes were tiny windows
wherein small children sighed in triplicate

i bring kisses of birds raised on rain
and exudation of muscadine
the princes of sky and cloud of the velvet prairie
the queens of the nacreous sea
and sufficient reason for a day

i am too old to wish the world round
small corners bang off into space
i am happy to pursue the remains of a waltz
written in rain on autumn leaves
the sun is coming up or going down
it does not matter so much as distant mountains
apprised through incense of campfires

but youth is the planting season
that succulent tribe of immortals
whose ungrown crops ripen tomorrow's suns
to you i would offer this darkening field of roses
and the wisdom of solomon
for a tincture of storm and one small breast of fire

Days Like These

fort bayard
(for larry godfrey)

in a fine spring rain
we shoveled shit into five-gallon buckets
from a pile big as a four-holer buick
while the mules who made this garden fodder
followed us back and forth to the car nuzzling and nibbling
convinced we were going to feed them
fine droplets of rain stood on their coats and eyelashes
as they wandered about like small ships in a green bay
or large lost women
when we drove away they stared at us as if we had never been
i like to imagine they were bereft
that we had somehow brought something to their day
and at home as we divided the spoils
i contemplated the nature of human happiness
whether the pure benison of manure
or the attention of fine mules

the mission

he hunkered on the porch
like a chicken caught in moonlight
and brought the words up like phlegm
through angry smoke and bad hair
his mother had sent him to borrow a bell from the neighbors
i wanted to say
-sorry kid
all my bells are busy right now-
or
-i just sold my last bell to the third prince of zanzibar for his wedding fete-
but he looked so small and wizened standing there
i invited him in for a cup of hot chocolate
and we talked for awhile about bells and star dust and the physics
of geriatrics while his eyes flew around in his head like tiny bats
-there is a science beyond bells- i said
-mom's loony as a pig fart- he said
and left my door with a belly full of hot chocolate
and the long strides of the innocent
trying hard to fit between the rain

Days Like These

the bird feeder

in islands of sky he is waiting
for birds to fall out of the air
like small handguns

there is a bruise of need in his eyes
as if your flying inaugurates
a chain of command authorizing breathing

the air feels like pudding
a friend with no bones
your feathers have their own addresses

as you circle
he is quiet as an elevator
like underwater rain in a foreign dream

his hands are small lost animals
his eyes drip suet
in his hair a garland of seeds

and as you begin to feed
he sings muscular songs
in the key of life

Tom McCoy

the cost of roses

the simplest of men
i sat in myself watching the wind
as day stretched from ear to ear
while the circus sang softly to itself
tightening tent ropes here and there exquisitely
as the elephants nuzzled each other like large ancient men in bad suits
and the guy in the top hat and tails walking back and forth
wringing his hands saying
-ladies and gennelman
ladies and gennelman-
when i saw his suit was stuffed with white rats nibbling vanilla wafers
and feared for the day
but just then the sun broke through the clouds
and i had to stand and grin and do a little dance
thinking what is the cost of roses to a man dancing?

Days Like These

fields of summer

sun works the garden like a bitch in heat

chlorophyll is a girl's best friend

summer is a kind of crying
long cells draw honey out of the hive
an age of innocence weighed in tomatoes
so hot the blood slaps in your head
like killer bees with hangovers

clouds gather but their voice is nada
i have seen more water in a third-grade pissing contest

but the fruit seems happy

birds bugger the cherries

the plums groan

i could build a house of pears

and the pure logic of flowers scuttles the mind
hollyhocks conquer vacant lots
iris slink in yards past all decency
poppies are tears of the sun
roses are cabbages of love
better than sex on a stick
sunflowers pull smiles up out of the ground
as the eye runs laughing like a child over the long fields of summer

Tom McCoy

prince of winds

where clouds bump the sky
and the sun goes kissing
lived a prince of winds

from his whistling realm airy minions
blew down the lone canyons of the heart
to the rude flower of the mind
honed their sharp hands
on the hard lives of men

that the prince loved that mad gift
the silvery high-breasted morning
was no secret
the birds
the gossiping trees
the worms in their holes rejoiced

but he knew only of wind
the wheel of seasons
the hurricane's lashing hair
the zephyr's gentle breath
the dust devil's dance

his friends were trees and grass
the golden poppies hemming the hills
berries of rain
the gliding birds of the air
the round sun's golden benison

but glib morning was the lover of all
she spread her favors among the world
never idling
always in passing her silver lips caressed
the eager and the dying alike
her kissing hands enfolding the lizard and the tree

Days Like These

the jealous prince held himself aloof
high from the world in windy silence
the clouds were lost
the dust grew roots
birds labored in the air
trees forgot how to talk
ships sat like hens on the listless seas
there was a stillness on the world
the world had not seen since it was young

and the sun came down like honey all around saying
-o thou prince of air
my sibilant and moving son
why this languishing of the elemental self?-

and the prince in his silence said
-father
my love is the morning
that silvery bright child of dew and laughter
but she heeds me not-
and the sun in his singing said
-o prince
know that morning is the child of night
born each day to delight poor man in his short and wintry span
wouldst thou hide the joy of man in thy covetous heart?-

and the prince in his pride said
-i care not for wretched man nor his trials
for i am the wind and move in my joy
i will have proud morning for mine-

and the prince in his fury strove to break the night
he howled and raged along the borders of evening
and into the abyss of darkness tossing trees
slamming rock and water to froth
churning the tired earth in his frenzy

until at last he lay spent gasping like a breeze
with no more breath than a willow
and slunk away like a whisper to his keep

and to this day
wind is no friend to man
when he rages at night and you are safe abed
think you only he is searching for his love
the morning
and hold yours the tighter

Days Like These

notes on the end of the world

the day the world ended
i was steady in my bones
away bent back upon itself
hard in the middle as a pelican's smile
under auguries of cloud
everything seemed summer
the skirling of anti-vivisectionists
wound among striking busts of lindbergh
and the virgin van gogh
and from down where the mangoes grow
under god's hairy thumb
it was like coming up out of a year's water naked
to where starry birds flew with st. flagellus
to the outskirts of martyrville
but mostly i remember tiny nipples of rain
and a girl who smelled like bells

expertise

if one thing in your life works
you are a fucking genius
whether king of toothpaste
or dalai lama of bladder control
to do one thing well is a pardon
a pass
a gap-toothed wonder
but all i could ever understand
was the sound of leaves
and holding hands in the rain

covenants

a man who drowned in the sun
was found floating near venus with a sly grin
covered in gold and lapis
dripping honey and turquoise
his heart had gone from a thumping thing to glass
in the breadth of a quark
and i have to believe he chose his swimming
as much as the moon flower chooses covenants of sun and soil
to live is a choice
to die is a living
so the soldier waits for the sun
rocking back and forth on his heart
like a gun

betty

she is sweet as onions
a gossamer child hovering in the mind
her need flows in waves
and we are swept beyond our shores
she is light as a sparrow's kiss
a feather of being
she glows like honey
with the exquisite rapture
of sea shells waking
she is a child swimming out to sea

o poor bankrupt butterfly
pinned to the struggling mattress
o skittery angel in a failing house
as you assume light
we begin to grow wings

Days Like These

attrition

a man of small equations
joe's life was sad as a bowling alley
breakfast was late and burned
his best friends were leaves
his children were bones and shells
his wife a turtle with pierced ears
his breath was rocks
his luck was a string in a hole in the ground
guarded by consumptive spiders
in his heart fierce crickets roamed

one day joe jumped into his god and drove away forever
without looking back
perhaps to the outskirts of mississippi
where he was attacked by kudzu and buried in persimmons
without holy unction of mustard or mayonnaise
the natives dawdling about their small dark teeth gnashing
like naughty fireflies with satan squalling on the death harmonica

such stories are instructional and bolster the young
but how to hold the faithful
when the sun comes up over the horse-heaven hills
like a harlot in a convertible?

a house in town

that the fault is mine i have no doubt
i so loved the simple sounds of evening
its blue sestina and soft quarrel of rain rinsing the hincty town
and the mouth of night leaning down

the river of my youth was wide
the far bank hung with myth and mirror
so i swam among myself
as the world rained down its plunder

there was a house in town
with less roof than bathroom
where we practiced lies and beer
and peed out the window on a fairy ring for good luck

oh to have discovered a new kind of kissing
found a cure for clowns
designed a hood ornament for large women
but never knowing i was king
the world talked and talked and talked
and i could never get a word in

Days Like These

soup kitchen

talking about death
is eating soup with a fork
you get a taste
but the essence is left
for the birds that gather
each morning for crumbs
and as they skitter across the snow
the cat behind the garbage can
twitches
and you wonder
what the birds
are talking
about

Tom McCoy

the janitor

as we slow
to our bones
the sun
is a sniper on the hill
life circles overhead
spinning the crowbright air
wheeling and laughing

now
i forget
faster than i learn
soon
i will be a broom
sweeping silent halls
of the heart

thieves

1

in the milk of my youth
it was morning all day long

white stones sang in the sun
beneath the holy streams

trees with birds in their mouths
called down the day

2

life falls down

lost in the heat of living
we lose our stickiness
and that feeling of falling
the ground rushing up like summer

the unsteady days wander like chickens
in a vacant lot
and we are thieves in our own homes

the novice

i dreamed jesus in thorns of honey
astride a great white swan
nibbling canned corn from a lotus blossom

the sun was pale candy

it is always thus

too late love loads the guns of light
falling on empty chambers of the heart
kissing too late or not enough
evoking the inchoate
like a face drawn on a napkin

i miss the child's itinerary
the pure product of the world
unkissed and uncrucified
wandering the self like a surrogate jew
lost in the endless hills of wonder

it is time for prayer and contemplation
the ritual of the ritual inflates the self
but i am empty as a bell
sweet jesus ring me loud
that i might know the time of thy passing

Days Like These

walt whitman

when walt whitman spoke
woke the dew on the rooster
he carved a heart in hilly country
down the drowning rivers of my youth

when walt whitman cried corn
the tasseled silk sang in the blonde valleys of summer
honeydews moaned for joy
watermelons rolled themselves to the porch
past furlongs of fertile girls

before walt whitman spoke
coughed up pieces of the moon
i could not conceive such a prodigious love
saying death thou art beautiful

old man of the mulberry shadows
sing down the slow asylum of years
come to the crossing
once again
tell me why i died

taking aim

it was a sweet gun
no taller than a short third-grader
pocked with age and patina of the innocent
the stock was cracked
held together by the iron butt-plate
and yards of black electrical tape

i can picture grandpa beating the-coyote-that-would-not-die
with it after it jammed
the moon a thin whisper on a night black as an asphalt apple

a knob-headed irish kid with brutal red hair
and the hands of a pumpkin picker
he hunted coyotes for school money
ears six-bits a pair
one ear zero

1903 winchester .22 semi-automatic
it won't shoot anymore
the chamber's split and the ejector's gone
it stands in the corner next to grandma's stuffed love birds
i use it to aim down the years

Part II:
Noon

Tom McCoy

Days Like These

willows

the earth will have none of me
were my intent stronger than a popcorn fart
i would have tomatoes bigger than basketballs
zucchini like godzilla's pecker
instead of apples wounded in their youth
villainous worms
and everywhere the sly chanting of birds

driven like a soft nail into a carpetbagger's dream
when i caught up with myself
i was through running
the trees were thinning
the year spinning to an end
as i practiced denouements on the patio
with one eye to the sky
but the sun
that old bad boy
just rolled around heaven

in the slow sentence of years
i have found more questions than answers
more reasons than stars
things have their own meanings
not everything has a reason
perhaps the willow is a willow
because it is not your grandmother

january

at the tire store
all the flats looked the same
air everywhere

in the parking lot under a dishwasher sky
sparrows goose-stepping
a dog buckled itself to my knee
and made coughing sounds

somehow i have traded the joy cookies for tofu
and the mild violence of believing
learning there is a fine line
between despair and grapefruit
that life wins its wings by learning not to fly
where boldly not to go
as love's bandit whoopee cushion sighs
until the world gets small
won't fit over

Days Like These

wet weather

once when the old car wouldn't start
i laid hands on the hood and wept for the frailty of man
then scraped the points with a jackknife
and drove off into the day
rejoicing in the utter blueness of the sky
the unction of trees
the sweetness of air
so when we pushed the car into the old gravel pit to watch it sink
as it sighed like a large unhappy third-grader
i was glad i saved for you the tarantula gear-shift knob
and those fingerbones that were under the front seat
grandma says they're good for wet weather

Tom McCoy

winter tale

we knew grief that winter
the roof died
the cow hung herself
jeffrey
the coughing dog
and i
ate the last deck of cards
at the time of the blue snow

next time
pretend you are cutting
my wrists

it might work

Days Like These

the dessert first

there is a peace
greater than groceries
kinder than rain
closer than kissing
purer than pissing

there is no dessert greater

and you will never be full
until it eats you

the wise

knowing more than we know
is a thing alive
seeing the fog through the fog
is more than caring for caring
as an exercise than love is fixable
the awful complexity of yes
the intellectual mud slide
the mystery of spiders
with legs longer than
the agility of supposed atoms
to weave life
and what the infinite smile
of a mountain
more than caring for
the mystery of spiders
weaving atoms into life
through the incus of infinity

who in hell among the wise
can gauge with impunity
the awful cost of turnips?

Days Like These

the record

by the lilacs
where the lawn sank
over the old cistern
we killed chickens

headless
they spiraled
pumping blood until empty
then collapsed on the burnished grass

my record was three laps around the stadium
a big busty old hen that had quit laying

merle declared it a foul
the regular pullets couldn't make two rounds

chicken heads piled like luckless rabbit's feet
startled voodoo eyes fading
pirate cats darting and swooping
the blue-eyed world
spinning away in the heart of a boy

the record still stands

but the sky holds a different wind
wearing a crown of feathers
and the time not come for plucking

**o la
love**

as we throttle through
these gut-shot lives
spring plucks a fuse
of fear

all about
some sister's firm fallopian curves
girls carry their legs like sonnets
in the hungry air

with the sun's guns going
and your body a sleek psalm
i wish to play salvation
a little

let us be gentle
o love
such time is rare

Days Like These

the stone boat

to love
is a lavish thing
a meal complete
a sweet sideways movement
a motion of music
in the nerve

(o spoilers
your love
is caves of roses
in summer hillsides
in the windless country
of your dreams)

be generous
with your gifts
consider yourselves
voyagers
in a stone boat
in a land
of sinking water

midnight kite

it was a baby-making moon
a grand bitch of a moon
claws deep in the night's flank

all about
the bones of the innocent
ticking like clocks

trees shimmering
like young girls

dogs trolling

in a moon breeze
two lovers
flying a midnight kite

composition 101

these words are fluff
nothing
do not read them
they are cheap
showy
don't waste
your precious
time

but
if you must look
look across the room at me
now

ah
your eyes
lady
your eyes
are pale forests
where among azure pools
fawns graze and legends roam

lady
i swear to you
nothing could be lovelier than
my balls on your chin

Tom McCoy

thinking of you
christmas 2001

this thought contains you and all the whirly natants
of the dexterous sea
yesterday's light and tomorrow's peanut butter
chickens of delight and the delicate leaf mold they shred
the ponderous sighs of elephants
the sounds of molecules mating
the horse on the hill and the turds he nonchalantly proposes
wind in the woods and the woods' idea of being woods
the death knell of stars divided by each snowflake
and the immaculately infinite permutations of composing love

Days Like These

the ace of strawberries

i am the ace of strawberries
a barn full of clowns
on your hard day

when you are sad
as rain on biscuits
i will clean your kitchen
sand your surface
and set you on a voyage of discovery

for you
i am fine underwear and fox skin gloves
buttered summer nights
in a forest of moons
watermelon pie

you are
good as groceries
a car that starts

your hands
have their own tides

Tom McCoy

doves

in this colony of the perplexed
the halls are adrift with somnolent dwarves
carrying kittens to the bewildered mines of being
paragraphs of homeless doves with eyes wide as the sea
a phalanx of mimes shuffling down the starved monkey season

their eyes are tragic caves where scared birds gather
to storms of violent impotence
small soft planets in orbits of pale flesh
with bones brittle as stars
hoarding the bitter dignity of silence

Days Like These

trees

trees are trains of green
charging through the storm
girls with no clothes on
with winter in their hair

filled with summer crows
or harvest moons
their beauty is the husk
and heart of childhood grown

when i wrestled trees
and ran with dogs
trees were trolls with rough skin
gods of green and sky

i swear
my knees would grin
if i knew now
what i knew then

Tom McCoy

observations at 55

in a forest of clowns there are no bumbershoots

the pelican is a large bird of saturnine countenance
whose wing bones make good hash pipes

clouds graze sky and give milk of rain

cats come and go but sex is a tax loophole

teenagers are doors with no handles that close mostly

coffee is an animal with tiny teeth that hardly ever sleeps

trees are slow moving people with bad hair that speak wind

i am an uncle of sorts with prodigious and mystical nose hair

there are many ways to squander but life is mostly delicious
and i have to go pee now

Days Like These

to a son

be not feasible
dot no i's
hold your heart up to the sky
like candy for the birds

live close to the bone
be a friend
get good at god
be president of pretend

love like a sailor's last night on leave
save a bit of yourself to throw away at need

weave your dreams
to keep you warm

slow down

the heart waits
for the mind to learn

late afternoon

with time's snotty dogs nipping your flanks
and gravity growing
the world conducts you like an experiment
all about are the petals of your life
scattered in a wind
you didn't even know was blowing
and your love
an unsigned letter
stuck to a fence in a vacant lot
in late afternoon

Days Like These

kildeer

1

he wanders like a starving rose
in shining rain
that slow sweet smile at half-mast
his love dangling like a broken arm
as kildeer dance in the mint-green fields

his eyes are the color of the wind
in his gnarled hands a child is singing
the melody breaks the bones of the heart
a lost martian lament
a phrasing of rain and elemental sorrow

2

the child studies the bee-fattening fields
green as giving
the ambrosial sun
the steady guest of wind

his eyes caress the elusive birds
the lyric leaping sky
as he opens his orphaned heart
to the dream-drinking world
the long chase begins

tigers

saw one on the way to work
on a day like yellow rain
eyes of black snowflakes
long white windy teeth

all day was tigers
the crouching secretary snarled
my boss had sprayed my desk
lunch at the local sandbox was claws and fur
with house dressing
afternoon of hiss and spit with occasional evisceration
so i was not surprised when i got home
to find one had eaten the smile off my wife's face

Days Like These

excerpts from the dogboy chronicles

be a butt sniffer!

ever want to piss on every tire in town?
dog every bitch to the ground?

the dog within behaves mostly
the occasional yelp and urge to urinate in public sublimated

but night
o dark and furless one!
in a forest of tall stars
mother moon will howl with me
in a fire of eyes we will taste the throat's blood
like smoke on lambs

who among you has not fought the urge
to take a good moonlight shit on your neighbor's lawn?

Tom McCoy

sailors and unicorns

1

with death come like a naughty sailor
to swab the longing from our dreams
i groan for gestures of unicorns
and the brazen kindness of apple trees

2

the mind is a sailor in a saucy hat
singing haloes to the wind
in a unicorn's skin is enough room
for all the golden soldiers of delight

3

in the beginning were sailors
dressed in sea chantys and glazed with morning
unicorns are blue under their clothing
like saints on fire

4

from sailor's lips dripped words of cobalt
the tincture smoldered in the sun
finding i could not feed all the unicorns
i sold the farm and moved to the world

5

sailors sun in their own time and no other
in the garage unicorns are rusting to azure
once
on a spring morning
i watched a robin eat a hummingbird
sailors eat unicorns because they can

seraphim

it's true
angels like twinkies
the angels in my closet are a noisy bunch
like a rainbow gathering of doves
i am sure such jubilance is commendable
but the neighbors look at me funny
i think they suspect me of harboring fugitive aliens or something silly
but when i tell them about the angels they smile and move away
steady as icebergs

it's a small closet
too small for so many angels
sometimes i wonder why they chose my closet
maybe it's a bus stop or waiting room or an elevator
i don't know
but they do like twinkies
they always eat the ones i leave
and i keep it real clean
never any dirty clothes or anything
i think maybe i'm a saint

Tom McCoy

conditions of longing

the rivers are mad with mermaids drinking blue tea
from the skulls of believers

i am lost as a sperm in an anus
living on the outskirts of the heart
on corn dogs and earwax in a nigger-colored convertible
with four left tires and wings so small it can barely fly

a foreign child at a sly wedding
following the strange animal of the self
into the cozening fields
as the soft eagle of the soul
flies vegetable loops of tatooed imagination

where the shining hieratic animals?
under a smooth star where all the cows live

i could never get lost in a woman again

Days Like These

bird watching

in terms of pure profit
the sun is up fifty points
the itinerant capital of spring
has swathed the land in apricots
the flawless sky is a lamb of blue
the air breathes in homeric couplets
you are a rocket of love
king of the glands
with all the pretty syllables of your life
gathered in avenues of rich shade
but still the small gears of earth
mesh the spirit's wheels
as milky children dance on the small feet of death
with the breathless walk of hummingbirds

love beyond star trek

when the dilithium crystals of your warp drive
are oozing anti-matter
and your photon torpedoes sag into the cargo bays
i will still love you

when all the meaty cows have left your pasture
and chickens gather to peck your grits

when the rubber chicken of your life
sags in the hallway like a bent broom

when time tucks in its heaven
and hitches off across the milky way

when we are sand
on some febrile spoon-fed yuppie shore
i will know your grains from all others
and still marvel
at the smooth smokeless motor
of your smile

elvis revisited

yeah
this is a soul jeep
4x4 astral v-8 with a/c and twin turbo jammers
jimmy hoffa's in the trunk
and my girlfriend's part angel and part cherokee
my house is right over there behind the trees
behind the wind
behind the sky

got a cigarette?
give us a bone
                eh?

i voted for nixon
y'know?

he was a quaker
the bonesucking farthead
don't trust them religionists
they'll gut you when the cross runs dry

bet you didn't know jesus was a dwarf
yeah
no bigger than a bounce
he ran out of funny money
so they hung him up like a pigeon to do the poo-poo dance
made an elvis out of him
colonel parkered the boy and left him to swing

but that's show biz
                        i guess
got a light?

Tom McCoy

no elephant graveyard

down by the viaduct
where the cars whiz by like piss bullets
and everybody is glad they ain't getting laid
cause listen
this winter must be paid for
the adjustable gauge of truly knowing
allowing the assumed to bloom like paregoric
in the mind's tree is sure as shit the way to breakfast
and this ain't no elephant graveyard
they die like candy wrappers
so go back and try again
leave your shoes by the door
with no breeze

and like a man looking up from a fall
i saw their words hanging like puffs from small cannons
in the torn vintage zeppelin air

Days Like These

monsoon

the rain came down like nipples in a sultan's dream
upon the drunken cactus
tarantulas like hairy hands fleeing their holes
and from cottonwoods drinking like sailors
a lizard's rictus grin
and the sand pocked like a randy adolescent
with ravens cursing in their black tongue
the air sweet as the after-dinner mint
we didn't pay for
at the dine and dash chinese restaurant
in seattle where the cook chased us down the ave
with his cleaver and we jumped a taxi to first street
and ran into the crowd at the market with the driver
cussing and waving his gun
and we made love in an old shower stall in the basement
as the rain sang in the streets overhead while we sank into each other
like drowning water

Tom McCoy

peanuts

eating peanuts in the dark
the last is the hardest
shuffling through the dry shells
like the empty backs of beetles
and the last fat one
like finding a poem
in the dregs of your old coat pockets
along with lint and bits of cough drops
the kleenex that you borrowed
and those three copper nails
left over from that pain-in-the-ass roofing job
the day that joe fell off the roof
into the rosebush
the foreman was pissed
and we laughed all the way to the emergency room
and that mouthy big-chested nurse says
-well look what the tooth fairy drug in-
and joe reached over and pinched her on the tit
and she slapped him and joe up and punched her
in the nose and it made a funny hollow crunch sound
like mouse bones breaking
sometimes peanuts are like that

possibly the last love poem

as if it were enough to know the enemy
when recent developments in quantum shoplifting theory
suggest a universe dangerously eroding its principal
by over-taxation and hyper-breeding
to the point that toenail clippings of truth
are more valuable than slivers of the true cross
and god is using rubber bands to hold up his socks
but still
after all the tents of our nights together
the intricate shores and bayous traversed
multitudinous rubber ducks and bathtub rings
climbing the everest of children
and the tangled forest of living
it's a wonder we still talk to each other
let alone hold hands and bark at the moon

Tom McCoy

awaiting velocity

i am awaiting velocity

the only breathing is being done by crickets
who hide like tiny sailors their infinite hearts in the harlequin night

papa is full of dying
an algebra of bones and tubes
a quandary of roses moving with the tide
where the sky walks on the wings of the sea
beyond the lever of words

papa
i wish you cartoons of light
velvet elephants in your stockings
and the tiny intricate hammers of love

baby steps

it's hard to remember when i first began to mistrust words
the enameled silence followed by skittery sounds
bird toenails on tile
dry broken kisses crawling slowly uphill
words like dishonest cows giving sad milk

the first word that bit me was *is*
a sharp little number in a hungover tune
squirming off the page
its bite was soft as ice cream
i bled ink slowly into silence
at home with the ripening tomatoes
the somnolent zucchini
the stolen heart making a sound
the small scared geese falling from the moon

Tom McCoy

homemade biscuits and blackbird dreams

grandma lives in the stick of herself
somewhere closer to love than all elves
from her whittled kitchen
biscuits rise to heaven
she is a child
swimming out to sea

grandpa lives in blackbird dreams
a deluxe prisoner of the mind
lost in the morning swamp of his loves
tadpoles swim back to sun-fed meadows
where a summer girl waits
with elves in her hair

they are frail wind-torn leaves
stuck to the wet sidewalks of the heart

but hooligan child
what of your parachute ways?
where all the buttery girls
the bright hills of morning?
gone as a sprinkle of sparrows
from a window sill

lover of old buicks and fine cats
a rumor wrapped in winter skin
dancing the sad dance of the one-legged frog
as time tucks us in

Days Like These

the race

no man undone
by the slow arc of the sun
i walk the smoking fields of day
like any fool
live quiet as a rose
hidden in the whirring world

life is the symptom
this season of the soul
retreating from grace
is the hardest race
god comes in dreams of old buicks
on angel wheels
steering like a junkie to the heart

sailor

i used to question what made me happy

is this adequate?
how can i maximize the air in this sentence?

now
when the chicken sighs
when the snail glistens
when the moth skitters
when the sky points up
i loiter lavishly in the space between spaces
slip like a skinny dolphin between the waves of want
sailing into the resonant sun
a sunset sailor who has never seen
an unhappy wave

Days Like These

sunday drive

when young is a country
you no longer go
and small birds gather
in the folds of your skin
and your face an address
you no longer know
and the lead in your pencil
has turned to sand
as you sloping stand
testament to gravity
beyond small boys and apple trees
and perfect the science of sighs
through a sea of sundays
as moronic nephews roll their eyes
and now
the long afternoon drive
the air is heavy
there are flies

Tom McCoy

housecleaning and the part-time zealot

o flaccid and desultory
saints of sameness
beware!
o bright corruption
frog-shaped longings
beware!
by the white heart of morning
i shall live clockwise
a circling man
in a garden of groan

by summons of salt
and backyard blessing
as love holds time in rocky bites
the walls of being are jericho bound
the sky is a fat blue purse
for a blessing of birds
where god is a flower
of many hands
to open the heart

ghosts of old gods
i need a shady angel
to take me for her lover pup
in a land of no coffee
with the sound of small streams
moving among white hills
and everything
everything
kissing

Days Like These

pale horses

she is lost as a loaf of bread
a cheshire child
moving in azure ways
down a summer country

do you remember my roses?

memories wander like mimes
down darkening hallways
joy lingers
like the kiss of bees
in her face
is the light of summer apples
the grace giving gives

a wintry sparrow
caught in the green horn of time
gliding past trees licked with rain

do you remember my roses?

death in her eyes
like two pale horses
drawn softly across the moon

if you listen
she will tell gently of bridges
of loves
how even the wind has thorns

cats dancing
(for josh and hunter)

of the many ways of being lost
i prefer bells of light and green hillsides apprised through rain
though your own proclivities may lead you through the tatooed universe
in search of the perfect search
i would see you with these essentials

days of cats dancing
electric summer moons
a pair of sunshine shoes
a woman who loves you more than salsa
hearts like home-grown tomatoes
tall mountains of the mind
oceans of summer evenings
and a soft ship to sail therein
clouds when you need them
friends finer than watermelon
may all your chickens be hens
and all your hens be happy
and when summer is over and all the hills are laughing
and the circus has left town
i will remember your great true hearts
and save for you a hole in the wind

Days Like These

hard morning

a chicken bigger than death sat by my door
as the weeds of summer soared and bound the clouds to the day
and though the sun strove to rise
that rooster crowed the day back to black
stripped the moon's gears
backed the sea up into a shell
the air dropped to the ground like dimes
as people halved and halved themselves saying
-see this great gift we are given
surely god loves us better than guacamole-
but the rain couldn't find the ground
and the frogs of morning pounded out their saturnine sorrows
trees held their breath and the balls of being were stretched like a string
over an outhouse door
when i killed that death chicken with one blow
and the world snapped back like charlie chaplin riding a bike backwards

Tom McCoy

rock soup

he took it from the canvas pack like a holy relic
a pocked glaucous thing the size of a calf's head
a veteran sworn to breathe life into the stew
bits of rabbit surfaced as he stirred the gray water
a carrot swam by
bits of sagebrush and dandelions
-smells like someone boiling a boot-
uncle just smiled
the sun whizzed across his teeth
-rocks don't lie-
he'd say
as morning walked off into day

Days Like These

the daily dog

daily sailing the sea of suction
to exercise this starving art
like a two-dollar whore with a rock-and-roll heart
puts the action in the unction
here love is best known by its lack
this level lawyered piece of ground
with dismal ratio prince-to-frog
where meaning is sold by the pound
and though the fleas be infinite
every day must have its dog

Tom McCoy

country fair

up on jump-off-joe
under a budweiser moon
we practiced sin
on anything soft
watched the town lights
winking through the warm night
below

how far back
through time's twisted sheets
does it go?
maybe mama
was a dime-a-dance dancer
daddy
a slick zoot-suit necromancer

it must have been
show time
here i am again
stretched out in this place
walking that walk
talking that talk
even
damnit
liking it here
still lost as ever a child
at a country fair

Days Like These

the death of miss cluck

she lay stiff as a dick
nuzzled between the fence and heaven
a hard white feathered pastry
with yellow feet

somewhere between love and duty
the chicken was left out
the coldest night of the year
twelve-year-old caring
was not enough to include a chicken
and i was remiss
in not checking the chicken checker

knowing a little guilt goes a long way
i don't blame the boy
but my unease is mounting
caught where no man should be
down to one chicken and counting

the christmas wreath

having out-danced death
he wore his prostate like an amulet
around his neck
a proclamation that looked like a pork rind

the gospel ladies were offended

-showed that sombitch-
he'd finger it and grin

when he was hit by a car
we were all kind of relieved y'know
but i liked old ben
he had spunk
he would probably like that i kept his amulet
every year about this time there's ben
hanging by the door with the fake holly and berries
rudolph santa frosty baby jesus and the whole bunch

Days Like These

the snowman

in a morning town on saturday
and the angles of the air just so
grace came down like snow all around
everywhere in the silly streets
and the children saw with children's eyes
the special snow and gathered round
and made a snowman out of sound
for his eyes they chose the sky
from a breeze they made his smile
in his hair was everywhere
from his nose a flower grows

as the children danced around their prize
the silly people stared
at the children-hearted empty air
and went home with their noses
but the children know
that when the world is gone away
only certain snowmen stay

Tom McCoy

new snow

we do what we do
knowing the ice is thin
knowing sunday never really comes
learning love in rituals of neglect
as things fall away

such easy infidels
lost to low gear and comfort of the world

somewhere south of wonder
i would be the utmost captain
of your cannibal kisses on a hobo train
o hear the lost and crazy bells of summer
sigh in the blue air

a vague child
i yearned for the yeast of the infinite
a maniac pizza with mystic sauce
a fool kissed by a white crow
in the tumbleweed of youth

until
subpoenaed by the world
when the meat-eating finger points
things fall away

the gears of her eyes
the good thick trees of childhood

as things fall away
we do what we do
from windy fields or bright bridges
perhaps finding at last the getting in the going
and turn to see the world
like a snowman snowing

Days Like These

plato's pants

imagine plato's pants standing lonely in a dark corner of the universe
and now imagine yourself a swan of immense proportions
a galactic swan finding and trying on those pants and walking across the street
to the snappy mart for a six-pack and some smokes
and now imagine being carded by the mustachioed lady behind the counter
that must be what death is like only smaller and with no beer

Tom McCoy

Part III:
Dusk

a summer thing

orphans of red balloons waved their juxtaposed hearts
in the city of nine candies
as flawless wenches labored over trenches of whitest licorice
to brew the sleeping king's dreams
while overhead winged scissorbills flew fandangos
heeding the chains of evening not

it was a summer thing
a time of swollen hoses and rainbow mists
burgeoning cells and heroic fecundity
hollyhocks swayed in a breeze reserved for minor gods or food critics

in that walled time
in that city by the moon
lived an eagle i loved
a jet whistle of a bird with blue feathers and spats
that flew bach cantatas wreathed in ecstatic cuban cigar smoke
i loved that bouncing bird like a son
but one day his enemies swallowed him whole
like an olive
and since that time my only consolations have been the sun in the morning
and the moon at night and girls in tight t-shirts

Days Like These

the winter child

nothing's the same
in this same old town
the children are coarse as gravel
answer only to money
they were never shown
the simple art of being alone

wearing rain for a hat
where hair used to part like wheat
i never planned
to be an old man
with breath like a hamster's butt
and ears like frying pans

the world was round and heaped
like a plate of leftovers

but
i am content
my soul has paid the rent
and i have a deal with dread
he does the books
i keep him fed

though times
i long for the smooth gear of yesteryear
and lost rivers of morning
smoking in the sun

children cut me with their eyes
moving in their soft bones
safe in their summer homes

early warning

if upon hearing the word *mature*
your scrotum puckers like a handful of potato chips
welcome

it begins with a love of polished places
refrigerators cry out in the night
sighing dreams of white in meaty rooms
nothing is lost
wheels turn in parables of moonlight
comets are kissing behind the couch
the big dipper lost its cargo long ago
heathens have invaded the sandbox
and the chrome virgins rerouted through tomorrow
eating fried angel sandwiches
as the whoopee cushion of your life
fills up time's silver buckets
the jaws of joy have loud crunch
far from the snap of money
and love's wet whistle
as the dream phone sputters
to answer is to sing beyond
where your bones are dancing a soft gun's song
in madrigals of moonlight
in a country on no color

Days Like These

forms of war

-flannel sheets
the honeymoon's over-
grandma said

can it be?
that great sticky god vanquished
by a few yards of nappy cotton?
the purest form of war pared to a touch?

but still my body moves with your body
there are as many ways to find us
as leaves in a witch's wind
as smoke rising through trees

to sail the sweet sea of morning
is an act of war
all forms of war have their anthems
let us be a song of brightening air
with no dominion

you said

hard by heaven in the geniustown
with the rifles of morning
aimed down the yelling years
you said
we are broken moons
moving over a sea of ragged hearts

once brave in a buick
with the world whining at the door
you caught a poem
and fattened it with sticks and bits of hope
as it sang softly
in the salty hollow of the heart

    -o child of tick
    son of tock
    dancing to
    the elvis clock

    child of rain
    son of ruin
    spinning in
    the spinning room

    prince of process
    on a scoundrel train
    part-time angel
    in a house of rain . . .-

we are god's kindling
burned in his image
you said
while waiting for the boy
with the houdini heart
the girl with magic thighs

Days Like These

such languid leaping dreamers
lined up like zeroes on a big check
lonely as integers
lost in a zen snow bank

we are like a desert
you said

Tom McCoy

where the free light falls

beyond opposites
where the free light falls
is a song unheard
a meaning with no meaning of ours
whose echoes are like golden leaves
falling in the heart
with the unutterable logic of rainbows

Days Like These

the dust suit

i am building a dust suit

the fine sediment sifts and settles
like old kisses in dark closets

no metaphysics
just the strop and hiss
of our daily sharpenings
the ablation of being
until the spirit is bigger than the box

and when you put it on
soft as the kiss of a rose
a shape where the feeling you were
becomes a small stitch in the wind
as if
on its way home
the sky tripped over you

orpheus depending

love is late
love is

boys
we are lost sea captains
sailing ancient seas

women arranging
women arranging
as flowers arrange the wind

love is late
is late

truth
is a small child
lost in a desert
pursued by tsunami

her eyes
are the headlights
in your mirror at night
gaining like a starving hound

Days Like These

bow hunting

the gut-shot boy in the back seat
the old man polishing his tumor
the child with half a heart
do not care if the moon sighs
in its velvet socket
that the early sun
is the color of first kisses
they only know
they are the arrow
and time is the bow

Tom McCoy

hollywood
the screenplay

there is a fire in the forest
that can't be put out

the animals are running
like peasants to a feast

their breath is winter in their throats

their eyes are watching in furious color
licking their lids with long strenuous summer tongues

in vast viscous industrial cauldrons
love is boiling

in volcanic envy the mountains are smoking

as all cameras converge on a squalid meadow
where stands a man
sharpening his penis
with a credit card

Days Like These

the task

lost in the hills of having
water slapped
out of my house
came a small fry
shaped like a spouse

wind is thunder
in the flinty hills
all the leaves clap
drown in wonder
or founder on fact

trees salute the breeze
birds dance on a wire
in the slow morning's wake
day conspires

this sensual loop of talk
draws the iron inch out
too often
i run when i should walk
in this part-time forever
where lies the true task of the heart

if you would stay
find the glory in the day

Tom McCoy

the saint

a boil among us
his mind swung to god
like an unplumb door

he slept the sleep of the blessed
while we thrashed and gnashed our futons

when we carved our livers in liquor
he drank from other cups

when we couldn't keep our derelict cars
between the ditches and bitches
the beamer of his life ran on rails

and yet he was happy in his ignorance
drinking only of the good
finding no want and a fullness of ends
so that when we ate him
we were surprised
he tasted like a man

Days Like These

the way back

i have come too far

the soul sags in its sack
a periscope in a pup-tent looking for a savior

my shoes long for other feet

ingots of self-contemplation line the shelves

there are no kittens here

the way back through the child
is a cave in a cloud on a windy hillside
where in mythic remembrance
broods the monstrous heart of spring

the nihilist retires

of things on fire
let them burn
the ash of contemplation
nurtures a dry soul
of things not
let them burn also
like salty kisses
in a skillet

seek the dry sea
the slow wheel's furrow
a wilderness of one

brother to fire
sister to dark
i was the first animal
on the ark

lulled by the heart's
soft haunted hammer
where smooth bones bless us
there are many kinds of kisses

light moves about a moving core
as i am less
light is more

the midnight garden

1

to live like ice
clear as prayer
pain sharpened to a kiss

in the midnight garden
cold weeds of the moon
invade the heart

the stars are white stones
in the dark stream of night

all about
the soft bones of intent
glisten like used smiles

2

slave to small vanities
i am undone by the least of sums

the salty tug of money
the smallest feet of children
the slow nose of rain

see
how clouds caress the moon's belly
softly
like two old lovers?

in a midnight garden
such blooms cannot hold
the dry sticks of the heart sigh

Tom McCoy

you would think
someone old as wing windows
would know
the hard cost
of planting roses in the snow

Days Like These

things shining

as we grow into our skins
life fills up
like deposits on artery walls
we look for meaning
where there is only rain
we must find solace
in trees
and sunlight off crow's wings
and things shining

Tom McCoy